D1366859

Fortune Telling

Fortune Telling

by
Margaret Baldwin

illustrated with photographs and drawings

Julian Messner New York

Manufactured in the United States of America

Design by Teresa Delgado, A Good Thing, Inc.

Library of Congress Cataloging in Publication Data

Baldwin, Margaret, 1948–
   Fortune telling.

   Bibliography: p.
   Includes index.
   Summary: Discusses "fortune telling" through the
use of tarot cards, crystal balls, palm reading, and
tea leaves.
   1. Fortune-telling—Juvenile literature. [1. Fortune
telling] I. Title.
BF1861.B27   1984   133.3'24   84-10826
ISBN 0-671-46135-4

Sep '87
13.00
Publ
c. 1

Acknowledgments

I would like to acknowledge the help of two people who have become very special to me—Sandra Baggett and Josef Luben of the Psychic Guild of Kansas City, Missouri. Their interest in this book and the time they spent working with me have been invaluable. I would also like to thank Fern-Robin for her generosity in granting me an interview. Sandra's children, Sarah Lynn and Lisa, were helpful in reading the text and offering suggestions as well as allowing interviews. I would also like to thank Jason Ladinsky, who added his comments from a child's-eye view.

Thanks, also, to the Kansas City Art Institute, who sponsors the Renaissance Festival yearly in Kansas City, for putting me in touch with the Psychic Guild. And, finally, I thank the Renaissance Festival of Kansas City, Missouri, for allowing us to take photographs for publication and for their enthusiastic cooperation.

MESSNER BOOKS BY MARGARET BALDWIN

Fortune-Telling
The Boys Who Saved The Children
Kisses of Death

(WITH PAT O'BRIEN)

Wanted! Frank and Jesse James

Photographs by Joellen Lewis
    Photograph page 73 courtesy N.Y. Public Library
    Picture Collection
Illustrations pages 13, 32, 69, 72, 83, 89 NYPL
    Picture Collection

Contents

Tarot:
An Ancient Picturebook

$\mathcal{M}$any famous people have been believers in the tarot cards. One of the most famous was the Emperor of France, Napoleon Bonaparte. According to legend, on the eve of the defeat that was to send him into exile to the island of St. Helena, Napoleon saw the sixteenth card of the Major Arcana—the Lightning-Struck Tower—turn up next to the card of the King of France. The Lightning-Struck Tower means destruction, defeat, the overthrow of governments.

Legend says this card turned up next to the King of France card before the Battle of Waterloo, where the French were defeated by the British.

In the opera *Carmen* by Georges Bizet, the beautiful gypsy girl, Carmen, is in love with two men: a soldier named Don José and Escamillo, a handsome bullfighter. Don José is very jealous of Carmen. He has deserted the army to follow her and has ruined his life, yet he feels he cannot live without Carmen. One day Carmen is watching her friends tell their fortunes with the cards. She takes the deck to tell her own fortune. Carmen is horrified when the cards reveal both she and Don José will die.

"I've read it aright . . . ." Carmen sings, "me first, then him . . .death for us both . . . the cards are true and will not lie."

At the end of the opera, Don José, driven mad by his love for the fickle Carmen, demands that she give up the bullfighter and come to him. Carmen refuses, although she has been warned by her friends that Don José will kill her. Just as Escamillo comes out of the bullring in triumph, Don José stabs Carmen. She dies and Don José is led off to his own execution.

The cards did not lie.

Unfortunately, this is all most of us know about *cartomancy*—the art of telling fortunes with cards. The fortune-telling cards are a standard part of every gypsy movie or story. Yet the *tarot* (pronounced taŕ-o) cards are much more than fortune-telling cards. They were originally designed, many people believe, for a more serious purpose. Their history is lost, however. No one is even certain where the word "tarot" comes from or what it means, although most think it is a word from the Hungarian meaning "card."

The tarot deck in use today contains seventy-eight cards. The deck is divided into three parts known as the *Major Arcana, court cards*, and the *Minor Arcana*. The word *arcana* or *arcanum* means "hidden" or "secret." The Major Arcana are the most significant cards of the tarot deck. There are twenty-one of them and they are the storytelling cards. The Minor Arcana consist of forty cards plus the sixteen *court cards* or *suit cards*. They are called court cards because they are made up of characters from a royal court; kings, queens, knights, and pages as well as the aces and other numbers. The deck of fifty-two playing cards you use today to play "Go Fish" or poker or rummy comes from these original fifty-six cards.

When you look at the tarot cards, you will notice first that they are cards with beautiful pictures of many different objects and people. Some may seem very strange to you. Each of these pictures tells a story to one who has the key to unlock its secrets.

THE KEY TO THE TAROT

In order to understand the pictures on the tarot cards we must first understand the use of *symbols*. A symbol is an object which triggers a thought in our minds. We deal with symbols every day. The words you are read-

An elegant Queen of Swords from an early French tarot deck. This is a court card in the Minor Arcana.

ROYNE · DESPEE

ing right now are symbols. As you read, the words form pictures or thoughts in your mind. Many other things can be used as symbols. A cross, for example, is a symbol of Christianity. A dove is a symbol of peace. A skull is a symbol of death. A skull and crossbones on a bottle are symbols of poison. These symbols are easy for us to understand because we see them every day.

Some symbols, however, are much harder to understand.

Do you remember what it was like before you learned how to read? You stared at those black marks on the paper and wondered what they meant. You knew they meant something to other people. Your parents looked at those marks and read you wonderful stories. But you didn't have the key that unlocked the mystery of the symbols.

Then you learned how to read. First you had to learn each letter of the alphabet and how it sounded. Then you learned to put those letters together to form words. Finally you learned to make the words form pictures and thoughts in your mind so that you, too, could read the story.

When you look at the pictures on the cards of the tarot deck, you might feel as if you haven't learned how to read yet. You see the beautiful pictures and you know those pictures are trying to tell you something. But you don't have the key.

In the early 1900s, *psychologists*—people who study how our minds work—discovered that some symbols mean the same thing to all people everywhere. These symbols are called *universal symbols*. The sun, for example, means light and warmth. A child is a symbol for one who is innocent, free from evil. The pictures on the tarot cards are also universal symbols and it is through these symbols that they tell their story.

The Minor Arcana
and the
Court Cards

*T*he Minor Arcana consists of forty cards plus the sixteen court cards. These cards are divided into four "suits"—swords, wands, cups, and pentacles (five-pointed stars). The swords, cups, wands, and pentacles are also symbols. Early man believed that everything in the world was made up of one of four elements: earth, air, fire, and water. In the tarot cards, the wand is a symbol for fire, the cup is a symbol for water, the sword is a symbol for air, and the pentacle is a symbol for earth.

Each suit in the Minor Arcana contains four court cards: a king, a queen, a knight, and a page. In our playing cards today we still have the king, queen, and jacks (the knight and page were combined), and we have four suits. But the swords became spades, wands became clubs, cups became hearts, and pentacles became diamonds. When the cards are used for telling fortunes, each suit is a symbol of one part of a person's life. The wands stand for home and family life, the swords stand for mental activity (thought and imagination), the cups stand for love and happiness, the pentacles (or coins as they are sometimes called) stand for business and money.

Besides the court cards, there are ten cards in each suit numbering from the ace (one) to ten. The tarot uses *numerology*—telling fortunes with numbers—as well as pictures to foretell the future. The number five, for example, is considered a divisive number. It divides

The seven of Wands from
two different tarot decks.

the numbers from one to ten. Five is a change in life, it is a point of no return. The fifth card in every suit is, therefore, a harsh card. The five of swords is thought by many to be the most severe card in the deck since the suit of swords is the suit of mental power. Many tarot readers say that the five of swords means death for a close friend or loved one. Nine, on the other hand, is a lucky number. The nine of cups is known as the "wish card" and is a very lucky card since cups is the suit of happiness and love. If the nine of cups turns up in a reading, it means the person will get his or her wish.

The pages in the court cards are message bringers. Any time a page turns up in a reading it means you will receive a message, a letter, a phone call. If it is the Page of Cups, you will hear news from someone you love or maybe even receive a proposal of marriage! If it is the Page of Pentacles (Coins), you might receive money.

The kings, queens, knights, and pages have other uses in the tarot deck. They can stand for the person having the reading done, the subject. They can also represent someone or something that will have an influence on the subject's life. If the King of Swords turns up in a reading, it could mean a strong-willed, intelligent man will play an important role in your life. Or the reader who is reading the cards for a dark, powerful man might choose the King of Swords to represent the subject. The pages are used for young people who are still in their parents' household. A page can stand for

If this card—the nine of Cups—comes up in a spread, the person's wish will be granted.

either a boy or a girl. In the castles of the Middle Ages, a page was a young man, usually of aristocratic blood, who lived in the castle training to be a knight and serving the nobleman who owned it—or even king and queen.

These are the cards of the Minor Arcana and the court cards. Now let's go on to the even more interesting Major Arcana.

The Fool's Journey

*T*here are twenty-two cards in the Major Arcana. They are numbered from zero to twenty-one. Zero is the "Fool." The Fool is the only one of the Major Arcana that is left in our modern deck of playing cards—we call it the "joker."

To understand the role of the Fool in the tarot deck, we must study the Fool's place in history. The cards in the Minor Arcana called "court cards" picture people from the royal courts of the Middle Ages: kings, queens, knights, and pages. In the royal court there was also a person known as the Fool. He was a clown, juggler, and jokester. He had a serious side, too. He was often used as a messenger or spy for the people in the court since he was considered too foolish to be a danger to anyone.

Generally, however, the Fool's duties were to keep the people of the court amused. The Fool made jokes about everyone in the court, including the king and queen themselves. This was to remind them that they were human, too, and could make mistakes like everyone else. Only the Fool could talk back to the king without fear of being punished. The Fool's jokes were often serious underneath. In the play *King Lear* by William Shakespeare, the Fool is the only one who dares to tell Lear he has made a tragic mistake when he angrily sends away the only one of his daughters who truly loves him.

"If you were my fool," the Fool tells Lear, "I would have you beaten for being old before your time."

"Old before my time? What do you mean by that?" the king asks the Fool.

"You should not have grown old before you got wise," the Fool answers.

The Fool was considered by many to be a very smart person underneath his clownish costume.

This is the Fool of the tarot cards. He is a symbol. Look at the picture of the Fool. A young person is walk-

THE FOOL .

The Fool on his journey.

ing on the edge of a cliff, a small dog beside him. The sun is shining brightly behind him. The Fool looks very happy. He carries a flower in one hand and a wand or staff in the other. At the end of the staff hangs a bag.

Now we are going to play detective and see if we can find out the hidden meaning of the picture on the card.

The Fool is you and I, every person starting out on the journey through life. This is why the Fool is number zero—the beginning. The Fool walks along the edge of a cliff showing that our journey through life will be dangerous. He has a friend with him, his dog. The dog stands for our *instincts*—those things we do without thinking, such as eating, drinking, running away when we are scared. Sometimes our instincts are good. They keep us healthy and protect us. We jump when we hear a loud noise in the dark and we feel our hearts pounding. Our bodies are instinctively getting ready to run away. But sometimes our instincts are bad. We cannot always run away. The dog can be a good instinct and save the Fool from falling off the cliff. But it might cause him to fall over if the Fool lets his instincts rule his mind.

The flower the Fool carries is white. It stands for the soul or spirit of the Fool. You will notice that, although the sun shines on the Fool, it is shining behind him so he does not see it. The sun stands for knowledge. It is the light which shines in our minds and drives away the darkness of ignorance and foolishness. The Fool does not have kowledge yet. Only when he finishes his journey will he see the light of the sun.

Can you guess now what the other twenty-one cards in the tarot deck stand for? If you guessed that they are people or events in the Fool's journey through life, you have guessed right.

THE MYSTERY

The tarot cards are pictures of all the stages we go through in life—from when we are very young and without knowledge like the Fool, to when we are adult, playing detective, trying to solve the mystery of life. The tarot cards will not help us solve the mystery. But they can make it easier to think about.

Let us look at the first person the Fool meets on his journey. This is the number-one card, the Magician. By studying the card we can understand the Magician's story. The Magician is standing behind a table. His right hand is held high, grasping a magic wand that is pointed toward the sky. His left hand points toward the ground. This means that the Magician draws his magic power from two places—heaven and earth. There is a symbol above the Magician's head that looks like an eight lying on its side. This is the symbol for *infinity*—

The Magician's story.

THE MAGICIAN.

time without end. If you look very closely, you will notice that the Magician wears a very unusual belt—a snake eating its own tail. This is also a symbol for never-ending time.

On the table in front of the Magician you see four objects: the four suits of the Minor Arcana—the pentacle, the sword, the cup, and the wand. Remember that these also stand for the four elements of the world—earth, air, fire, and water. The Magician is dressed in long robes. If you could see this card in color, you would see that the robes are red and white. The flowers around the Magician are also red and white. The red flowers stand for our desires: things that please us or make us happy—like good food, money, presents, friends. The white flowers stand for soul or spirit, the things that please us in different ways—like our religious beliefs, listening to music, looking at artwork. (It was a pagan custom to use flowers to break spells—like the evil spell of sickness. We follow that ancient custom today when we send flowers to people who are sick.)

The Magician is the first person the Fool meets on his journey. What the Fool learns from the Magician he will need all the rest of his life. The Magician tells the Fool—and therefore all of us that we can all be Magicians. Our magic is the magic of the body and of the spirit. This magic rules the elements of earth, air, fire, and water. The Magician tells us that in order to make our own magic, we must open our eyes and see the magic all around us and inside us. This is the first lesson we learn in life. There is magic inside of us, magic in our bodies, magic in our minds, magic in our souls.

The Fool meets many people on his journey. He sees many strange things. Each one teaches him something about himself and life. The Fool will meet an Emperor and an Empress, a man driving a chariot, a woman taming a lion, a hermit carrying a lantern. He will meet death and a devil. He will see a tower struck by lightning. He will see a star, the sun, and the moon. Each of these cards tells us something, if we have the key to understand it.

This is the mystery of the tarot cards. The pictures on the cards are solved through understanding. You will understand some of them now and more as you grow older. As you get older, you add new words to your vocabulary. In the same way, if you keep studying the tarot cards you will find that when you are an adult many of its secrets will be open to you.

Does everyone understand the tarot cards completely?

Probably not. There have been many books written, trying to explain the secrets of the cards. The biggest mystery is still where did the cards come from in the first place? Who drew the pictures and why? Until we can answer those questions, we will never know for certain all the secrets of the tarot.

Picturebook from the Past

$\mathcal{A}$ long, long time ago, in a time we have forgotten, a group of the very wisest men and women met together. They were the priests and priestesses of a very mysterious and powerful religion. They had come together because they foresaw a great darkness falling over the earth and they knew that their time was drawing to an end.

"When we are gone," said the High Priest, "all of our knowledge will die with us unless we can think of some way to pass it on."

"It must lie hidden through the Great Darkness," the High Priestess warned, "or else it will be destroyed and lost forever."

The priests and the priestesses thought long and hard about this matter.

"We will paint the symbols of our wisdom on a huge building," said one of the priests. "That way it will last forever."

"No," said the High Priest. "Buildings can be destroyed. That will not work."

"We will carve the symbols of our wisdom on gold," said a priestess. "Gold does not rust. It will last forever."

"Thieves will steal the gold and melt it down," said the High Priestess. "That will not work."

"We will tell our secrets to one man who is wise and honest," said another. "Before his death, he will tell one other and so on. Thus will our secrets be kept safe through the Dark Ages."

"Every man has his price," said the High Priest. "We cannot be certain this person would not sell our secrets."

Everyone sat silent and gloomy. It seemed there was no way their wisdom could be passed on. Finally the youngest priestess among them spoke up shyly.

"Nothing is hidden so well as that which is in plain sight," she said. "Let us put the symbols of our wisdom on playing cards and tell men they are meant for nothing more than games. After the Dark Ages pass, there will come those who will be able to understand our symbols and thus will gain from our wisdom."

The High Priest and the High Priestess nodded and all the others agreed that this, indeed, was the best way to keep their wisdom safe through the Darkness that was coming. And so the tarot cards were born.

This is just a legend, one of the most popular legends about the tarot. But no one knows for certain. The beginnings of the tarot cards are lost in the dark shadows of time.

In 1392, Charles VI, King of France, paid an artist for three decks of hand-painted cards. Some of these beautiful cards still exist and are on display in a French museum. The designs look very much like those on the tarot cards pictured in this book. They were painted with paint made of lapis lazuli and strange powders of "dragon's blood" and "mummy dust," and were trimmed with gold. There are some who think the artist, Jacquemin Gringoneur, made up the cards himself. However, Gringoneur was interested in *astrology*—the predicting of the future by the stars—and also in the *occult*—the study of that which is hidden from the eye or the understanding. He had therefore already seen many fortune-telling cards whose designs he probably used.

About twenty or thirty years later, in the early 1400s, Gypsies roamed through Europe. They brought the tarot with them and, perhaps for the first time, showed the Europeans how to use the cards to tell fortunes. No one knew where the Gypsies came from in the beginning—not even the Gypsies themselves—and the Gypsies could not remember where their ancestors first came across the cards. It was certain they did not make up the cards. They told fortunes from the pictures, saying whatever they felt as they looked at the pictures without going into any deeper meanings.

The Church of the Middle Ages was very much against the cards, for use as games and for fortune-telling. They tried time and again to get rid of them, and we find early laws in various parts of France and England banning cards and forbidding card games. Thus only a few people knew about and used the cards. These were the very rich who could afford to have the cards painted and who could play with them without

"With three cards I will be glad to tell you about all the happy and unhappy events of your life," says the fortuneteller in this old French engraving.

fearing the law, and the Gypsies who knew no laws other than their own. Witches and warlocks and wizards of the Middle Ages used the cards to work their magic. And oddly enough the Church kept and studied the cards. Believing they were tools of the devil, they thought it best to know just what the enemy was up to. The tarot cards today contain many Christian symbols. You will find angels and monks, and one of the Major Arcana was known as the Pope in early decks. (It is now known as the Hierophant.)

When printing with movable type was invented in the late fifteenth century, the cards could be printed so that everyone could own a deck, not only the rich. Card games became very popular and the Church fought against them without much success. The Christian symbols on the cards may have been put there to try and make it easier for the Church to accept them, or they may have been added to the cards because the Church was so much a part of everyone's life.

For many centuries the cards were used only for games, fortune telling, or to work the secret spells of the wizards. It was not until 1781 that a book was published showing that, at last, people had learned to understand the deeper meaning of the tarot. This book was written by Antoine Court de Gebelin, a French *occultist*—one who studies the occult sciences. He stated that he believed the Gypsies had come from Egypt. The English word "gypsy" comes from the word "Egypt." The English thought the Gypsies looked like Egyptians. Actually, scholars today have evidence that the Gypsies come from India or Asia. De Gebelin claimed that the tarot deck was a book of hidden knowlege from ancient Egypt. People believed that the Egyptians had been able to do many wonderful things such as change any cheap metal into gold. The tarot cards were supposed to teach these things.

After this there was great interest in the tarot. Many people tried to explain their secrets, and are still doing so today. The cards have been traced back to almost every great religion from Christianity to that of the ancient Greeks, Romans, Egyptians, and the religions of the Far East. They have been said to come from the Hebrew *Kabbalah*—a mystical method of interpreting the Scriptures to foretell the future. Major Arcana compare with the twenty-two letters of the Hebrew alphabet.

No one knows. Whatever its origins, it would seem that the tarot is the story of humankind.

5

The Reader Today

$\mathcal{W}$e have seen that the tarot cards tell a story. How do they tell the future?

First, to say that the cards predict the future is not exactly true.

Josef Luben is a member of the Psychic Guild of Kansas City. He has been reading the cards for twenty-eight years and teaches classes in tarot reading.

"The cards do not 'tell the future' as so many people believe," Josef says. "The cards tell what path you are on in your life now, much as the Fool learns about himself on his journey through life. When I read the cards for

Josef Luben, dressed as a wizard for a Renaissance festival, carries a pet white rat—as wizards of old often did.

you, I will tell you a great deal about yourself and where you are going, what you are doing with your life now and what you can do with your life if you continue on the path you are walking."

"Can the future be changed?" I ask.

Josef laughs. "Yes. The quickest way I know of to get someone to change is to tell them what they are going to do!"

For an example, we can look back again at the story of Carmen. She saw death in the cards and she sang, "In vain you shuffle . . . the cards are true and will not lie." She believed that she and Don José *must* be killed. But, although the cards foretold death, there were many things Carmen could have done to avoid it. She could have married Don José. She could have packed up and left town. Carmen was in control of her life—she could have walked another path.

"Will the cards answer questions?" I ask Sandra Baggett, another reader and also a member of the Psychic Guild.

"Yes," Sandra answers. She shuffles the cards. "Ask a question."

"I have written a novel," I say. "Will it ever be published?"

Sandra lays the deck of tarot cards face down in front of me and tells me to cut the cards with my left hand, dividing the deck into several stacks. I do so, and then put the deck back into one pile. Sandra takes three cards off the top and turns each one up so that she can see it.

She studies the cards for a while.

"Yes," she says finally. "The novel will be published but only after a long period of discouragement and frustration."

Sandra Baggett laying out the tarot cards.

When you go to a reader you sit across from each other at a table. Sometimes, depending on the reader, there will be a black cloth spread on the table. Many readers believe that the black cloth keeps away unwanted powers or spirits that might affect the cards. Most readers keep their cards wrapped in silk in a wooden box. They believe that this, also, keeps them protected from outside forces. Readers often have a very close relationship with the cards. Many put a new deck of cards under their pillows at night to add to this closeness. According to Josef Luben, some readers even cast spells on their cards which could make anyone else handling them carelessly feel sick and dizzy.

Other readers, however, are more matter-of-fact. Sandra just spreads the cards out on the dining room table. I ask her about the black cloth and if she keeps her cards wrapped in silk.

At a reading, Sandra and a client face each other across a table spread with a black cloth.

"No," she answers. "I keep the cards in a box mainly to protect them from people, not outside forces. Tarot cards are expensive and I need a new deck every three or four months. I don't want them falling in the soup or the kids playing with them and losing them. I don't need the black cloth or the silk wrapping to feel close to my cards. I think some readers just do that to please the subject. People have seen the cards read in movies and they don't feel right without all the extras."

Josef Luben doesn't agree with Sandra. He tells his students to sleep with their cards under their pillows, wrap them in silk, and keep them in a wooden box when not in use, to treat them with respect.

"The only link between the reader and the person he or she is reading for is the cards," Josef teaches his students. "If the cards have been disturbed by some outside force, you may find that you do not give a good reading. Handle your cards a lot, even if you are not reading them. Shuffle them while you are resting, watching television, or just sitting and thinking quietly. Keep them safe. Do not allow anyone to handle your cards—except the person you are reading for—especially if it is a person who upsets you."

The person having the cards read is called the *querent*. Querent means "one who inquires or asks a question." The reader and the querent should be in a quiet place where they both can concentrate. The reader closes his or her eyes and reshuffles the cards. Sometimes the reader will call upon God for wisdom. Mainly what the reader is doing is freeing the mind to be receptive to the feelings of the querent.

"A good reader knows himself or herself," Josef Luben tells his students. "Only if you know yourself and you are comfortable with yourself can you tell other people about themselves. Every reading you do has a lot of yourself in it. When you close your eyes and shuffle the cards, you are clearing your mind so that it opens up to your own feelings and also those of the querent."

The reader begins by choosing one card to represent the querent. This is the *significator* card—the one that "signifies" or "stands for" the person having the reading done. The selection of this card is usually up to the reader, although there are traditional rules to follow. One of the queen cards is generally chosen for a married woman, one of the king cards for a married man, and one of the page cards for young people still living with parents. The reader might want to choose a knight card for a young man in the military or the emperor card for a politician.

Once the significator card is chosen, the reader either lays it face up on the table or puts it back into the deck, depending on the type of reading. The reader then asks the querent to either shuffle the cards, cut them, or simply lay his or her hands upon them. It is by touch that a link is formed between querent and reader.

The reader then takes the cards and lays them out face up in a pattern called a *spread* since the cards are spread out upon the table. There are many, many different kinds of spreads. A spread may use no more than

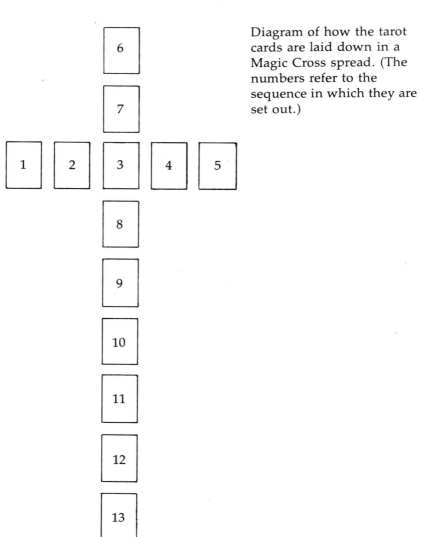

Diagram of how the tarot cards are laid down in a Magic Cross spread. (The numbers refer to the sequence in which they are set out.)

three cards or all seventy-eight. It is up to the reader. A reader may even work with two or three different spreads to give a complete reading.

The reader may ask the querent to concentrate upon a particular question or problem the querent wants answered. Once the cards are laid out, the reading begins.

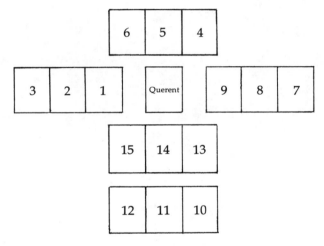

Diagram of a Wish spread, used when the querent wants to know if something special will or will not happen.

How the Cards Are Read

*H*ow do readers read the cards?

Besides telling a story, each of the seventy-eight tarot cards has a *divinatory meaning*. The word *divinatory* comes from the verb "to divine," which means "to foretell the future." The tarot card reader *divines* the future by studying the cards. The divinatory meaning of the cards is different from the symbolic meaning of the cards, although it is sometimes very close since it is directly related to the pictures on the cards. The reader knows the meaning of each card. He or she must, however, interpret the card according to (1) whether the card falls right-side up or reversed, (2) where the card falls in the spread and (3) the reader's own feelings.

Unlike an ordinary deck of playing cards, tarot cards have a top and a bottom. If, as the reader is laying out the cards, the card lands with its picture upside down, this gives the card a different meaning. Some readers say it completely reverses the meaning of the card, others say it merely lessens the meaning. If the Fool, for example, appears right-side up in a spread, it means that the querent is a dreamer. He or she is working toward a great goal and may be about to act unwisely since the Fool tends to act without thinking. The reader will probably warn the querent to be careful and think through any decisions. If the Fool lands upside down, however, the reader may interpret this to mean the querent is behaving foolishly and warns that any decisions he or she makes will be unwise.

The upside-down Fool has a different meaning than if it had fallen right-side up.

The Magician card landing right-side up means that the querent is creative, with a strong will that can take ideas and turn them into reality. Upside down, however, this card means the querent is weak willed and the creative power may be used for evil purposes. Other readers, however, believe that if the card falls upside down, it only lessens its effect. These readers would interpret the upside down Magician card as a sign that the querent has creative powers but must work hard to use them.

Reading the cards is a very personal matter for the reader. Each reader must choose to read the cards in the way that suits him or her best. Every reader is different, so every reader will see the cards a little differently.

THE SPREAD

Where the card falls in the spread, and the type of spread used, also affects how the reader will interpret a particular card. To understand this, we have to look at the various kinds of spreads.

Some spreads are simple, such as the "Gypsy spread" or the "Yes/No spread." These use only three cards.

"I like this kind of spread when I read cards for young people," Sandra says. "It is difficult reading cards for youngsters. Some readers won't read the cards for anyone under sixteen. Young people are so involved with their families that when you do a reading for them you always end up with a lot of family problems. Most of my readings for young people are at fairs and festivals where they just come for fun. They want to know if they'll be asked to the prom or if they're going to pass English this semester. This type of spread answers those questions easily for me."

5	4	3	2	1

FUTURE   PRESENT   PAST

A very simple yes-or-no spread may have 5 cards instead of 3.

The first card is chosen by the reader to represent the querent—the significator or the "S" card. It is placed face up. The next two cards are drawn by the querent from the deck which he or she has already touched or cut. These two cards are placed face up to the right of the "S" card. The first card, according to Gypsy tradition, tells the querent what is happening in his or her life now. The second card is a person he or she will meet, or something that will happen in the future.

"What would you tell the querent if you saw danger in the cards?" I ask Sandra.

"If I see danger in the cards, I warn the person," Sandra answers. "But it isn't like you see in the movies. I can't look at the cards and say 'two weeks from Thursday you are going to step out into the street and get hit by a bus.' I do, however, seem to have a sense about danger and cars. Lots of times I see danger for someone and I'll have a feeling it has to do with their car. I warn them to have their car checked. Sure enough, they'll call me and tell me they found the brakes were going bad or a tire was getting low."

"What if you see death in the cards?"

"No reader should ever tell the querent there is death

A tarot Death card has many meanings.

·DEATH·

in the cards," Sandra says. "That is often misunderstood. The 'Death' card in the Major Arcana doesn't necessarily mean death for the querent. It means death of a way of life, maybe, and the beginning of something new. The future can always change. I've never seen death for the person I'm reading—although Josef has. I have, however, seen death for people around them. There are times when I see serious illness or accidents. I tell people to go to the doctor for a checkup or quit driving recklessly or get off drugs. If I see danger in traveling, I tell them maybe they should consider going by car instead of the train or plane they planned to use."

THE CELTIC CROSS SPREAD

More complicated spreads reveal more details about the querent to the reader. One of these is known as the "Celtic Cross spread" or the "Grand Cross." It is very popular with readers and is fairly simple for a beginner to learn. After the "S" card is chosen and the remaining cards shuffled, the deck is laid face down before the querent. The reader asks the querent to cut the cards into three piles using his left hand. The left hand is used because it is the hand closest to the heart. In palm reading, the left hand also tells the future. The querent is then told to restack the cards in any order, using the left hand again. The querent returns the cards to the reader who takes them and begins laying out the spread.

The "S" card is laid down in the center face up. The first card drawn is laid over the "S" card. This card is said to "cover" the querent and tells about what is happening at the present time in his or her life.

The second card the reader draws is laid across the "S" card. This card "crosses" the querent and tells of opposing forces, good or evil. According to some, this card should always be read face up.

The third card is placed below the center cards. This is what is "beneath" the querent—those ideas or events that are behind or in the past.

The fourth card is placed above the center cards. This "crowns" the querent and tells what lies ahead, and hopes and fears.

The placement of the fifth and sixth cards depends on which way the picture of the "S" card is facing. If the "S" card is a queen card and she is facing to the right, then the fifth card is placed to her left since this card represents what is "behind" the querent. The sixth card is then placed to the right—the direction the queen is facing—and this is what is "before" her.

We have now formed a cross, with all sides equal.

The seventh, eighth, ninth, and tenth cards are "future" cards. They are placed to the right side of the cross in a vertical line. The seventh card at the bottom is the querent's overall future. The eighth card is future home life, the ninth card is future hopes or fears, and the tenth card answers a specific question or is the final outcome of a problem.

When the cards are spread on the table, the reader studies them, laying the rest of the deck aside. The reader may ask the querent to concentrate upon a specific question to be answered. Then the reader turns up the first card and interprets it, telling the querent about the present. The reader moves to the second card—the one lying crosswise—and interprets it and then moves on through the reading, telling the querent about the past and what can be expected in the future in terms of job, family, money, success, travel plans, dangers, hopes, and fears. If the querent has a particular question to be answered, the reader will try and answer it at the end of the reading.

"What kinds of questions do people ask?" I ask Sandra.

"Most people come to me with questions about money. They want to know if they should invest in the stock market, for instance. I can answer that from the cards, but sometimes they want me to name a stock to put their money in! I can't do that. I don't know anything about stocks."

"Do you tell them you can't do that?"

"Yes. It is important to always tell the truth."

"What else—love and marriage?"

"People ask questions about their health, either their own or that of someone they care about. And perhaps then about love and marriage. It is different with each reader. I just happen to be particularly good about business investments and cars. I know readers, though, who are excellent at predicting marriages, divorces, births of children."

Sandra often uses two or three different spreads to get an overall view of the cards. She can see if the same things turn up in different spreads. A serious reading takes about an hour, although there are some very complicated spreads that take several hours.

"What is the most important thing to you about being a tarot card reader?" I ask Sandra.

"Always tell the truth," she answers.

Going to a Reader

*Y*ou say you always tell the truth," I continue my conversation with Sandra. "What if someone asks a question, and the cards don't tell you the answer?"

"I tell them I can't answer it," Sandra says. "That happens sometimes. There have also been people I can't read the cards for at all. I lay the cards out and I get nothing, no feeling at all."

"What do you do?"

"I pick the cards up and tell them I can't give them a reading. I suggest they try another reader."

"According to the Gypsies, the customer must always 'cross the gypsy's palm with silver' before a reading. Do you believe the reader must be paid or the reading isn't worth anything?"

"I believe the reader *should* be paid, if only for his or her time. I do readings for free, though, if someone is really in trouble, wants my help, and can't afford to pay me."

"Do you read for your friends?"

"I do, but I don't like to. Sometimes I know what my friends want and I want it for them so much that I read things into the cards that aren't there. It is much better reading for people I don't know."

"What do readers charge for a reading?"

"It isn't a charge so much as a donation for the reader's time, and it varies. A reading may take 30 minutes or two hours. The donation could be $10.00 or $50.00. It just depends on the individual reader. At fairs, it is cheaper—maybe just a few dollars. People only want short readings. They go just for fun. I enjoy working festivals. I can give a person a good reading in just three or four minutes."

"Where would you go to find a good reader, one you could trust?" I ask Sandra.

"Just for fun, I'd go to Renaissance festivals or a Psychic Fair. Most major cities have them now."

Sandra travels all around the country going to Renaissance Festivals. People dress in costumes from the Renaissance period and there is usually a king and his

Dressed in Renaissance costumes for a fair.

court with princes, princesses, and knights, jugglers, and fools. Jousting tournaments are held for the knights. There are magic shows with wizards and sorcerers, beggars walk the streets and there are, of course, fortune-tellers. Sandra continues, "You could also call the Psychial Society if they are listed in the phone book. Occult book stores usually have listings of readers. But remember, some readers will not read for anyone under sixteen."

"How often do people come to you for readings?"

"It depends on the reader," Sandra answers. "I like to read for people once every three or four months, but generally not more often. If someone has a problem or a question they want answered immediately, I will read for them. Some readers, though, will read for a person only once a year."

"How did you start reading the cards?"

"I began about twelve years ago. I was going through a rough time in my life. I was feeling really low and there was nowhere to turn for help. I bought a deck of tarot cards because I liked the pictures, I was attracted to them. I checked out some books from the library and began reading about and studying the cards. I started reading for myself and I discovered they helped me. Learning about the cards, I learned about myself and I came to grips with some of my own problems. Finally I found out that once I had come to know myself I could begin reading for other people."

"Did you take classes?"

"No. I didn't take a class on reading the cards until I had been doing it for several years."

"What do people say when they find out you are a reader?"

"Most people are very curious about it and interested in the tarot cards." Sandra laughs. "It's a great way to liven up a dull party. Seriously, though, some people are frightened of it or they disapprove."

I talked to Sandra's daughter Lisa who is in junior high school.

"What do the other kids think about your mother being a tarot card reader?"

"Most of the kids don't know it," Lisa says shyly. "I don't talk about it. One girl found out, once, and she told me my mother must be a witch."

"Can you read the cards?"

"No," she answers quickly. Then, "Well, just a little."

"Children make good readers," Josef Luben told me. "Their minds are very open to new concepts and to the symbols on the cards because they don't have any fixed ideas to get in the way. The biggest problem they have is that the cards are very complicated to memorize."

It was interesting going to a reader. A lot of what Sandra told me about myself was true and it was certainly fascinating to watch her lay out the cards and read from them. You can go to a reader *just for fun*. You might learn some interesting things about yourself!

As for what Sandra predicted about my future, I hope it comes true. I hope my novel gets published!

But—do tarot cards really predict the future?

Crystal Ball Gazing

*T*he art of crystal ball gazing is very old, probably almost as old as humankind. We have records which tell us that primitive people looked into pools of clear water to get answers about the future. They saw pictures in the water which were studied for their symbolic meaning—like the pictures on the tarot cards. A Native American who looked into a pool and saw a buffalo, for example, might take it as a sign that his tribe should begin hunting. It is not easy to carry pools of clear water around with you all the time, however. After glass was invented, people began looking into clear crystal globes to see images they could interpret into visions.

The ancient Greek oracles—those who foretold the future—used crystals to foretell events. The most famous oracle was at the temple of Apollo at Delphi. Rulers and generals and ordinary citizens came from all parts of the country to question the oracle before planning any major event. In other parts of the world, priests wore crystals on golden chains around their necks. They believed they could communicate with spirits through the crystals.

While amost anyone can learn to read the tarot cards or palms or tea leaves, it is very difficult for someone who is not a *clairvoyant* to read a crystal ball. The word "clairvoyant" means "clear sight." A clairvoyant sees things that are not visible to anyone else, like pictures in a clear crystal ball. These pictures come from the clairvoyant's mind and are interpreted by him or her. The ability to see images in a crystal ball is considered a very special gift, one not many people have.

Aurora—a crystal ball gazer.

Fern-Robin is a crystal ball gazer. She does not want publicity.

She explains. "Once a newspaper did a story on my mother and me. It was a good article. The reporter was very interested in us. But it caused trouble. People in our church told us we could not come to church anymore. They said we were witches, tools of the devil."

"Do you believe that?"

"No! My mother and I believe that our gifts of clairvoyance are gifts from God."

Fern-Robin is a fifth-generation *psychic*—a person who is sensitive to forces beyond our physical world. "Years ago, my great-great-grandmother was taught the art of palm reading by Gypsies who discovered she had a natural psychic ability. Palmistry has been handed down in our family. My mother is very good at it. She can read palms and she can not only tell you what the lines mean but can see images in her mind about you. She amazes people with her skill."

"Did she teach you to read palms?"

"Yes, but I'm not as good as she is. She can't read crystal balls, though."

A true clairvoyant sees pictures in the ball. How or why, we do not know. There are those who believe that this skill can be learned by much study and concentration, if a person is not born with the ability. Fern-Robin, however, was born with the gift.

"When I was a small child, I'd meet someone and I'd see a picture over the person's left shoulder. I didn't know then that this picture was trying to tell me something about that person. I didn't think much about it. I thought it happened to everyone. Then my mother found out and told me it was a very special gift."

"Did she teach you to read the crystal ball?"

"No. She never used a crystal ball. She began teaching me fortune-telling using the fortune sticks. These are sticks with pictures and numbers on them. You toss them into the air and tell fortunes by the pattern they form when they fall. When I was older, she taught me to read palms. I kept seeing pictures but neither of us knew how to use this gift."

"When did you learn?"

"It was during a troubled time in my life. I was going to a friend for help and counseling. I told him about seeing pictures and he immediately said I should be using a crystal ball. Sure enough, I could see pictures or images in it right away. I learned to interpret the images—to understand what they meant to me and what they were trying to tell me about people who came to me."

We sit together in Fern-Robin's living room. The crystal ball stands on a small wooden stand in the center of a table covered with black velvet. The crystal is beautiful—very clear and smooth and round.

Aurora consults her crystal ball. She sees good things for her client!

"The crystal must be kept clean," Fern-Robin says. "No one is ever allowed to play with it, although I do let people touch mine. It looks very cold, but sometimes it is quite warm to the touch."

A heavy smell of incense fills the air. I sit on a couch, one of Fern-Robin's cats next to me.

"The cat always sits next to the person I'm reading for," Fern-Robin tells me. "No matter what she is doing or where she is, when I start a reading, the cat joins me."

The cat sits next to me the entire time. I play with her while I talked to Fern-Robin. When it is time for the reading, however, the cat suddenly sits up and stares into the crystal ball.

"I wonder, sometimes, what that cat sees," Fern-Robin says. It is very quiet. Fern-Robin sits with her eyes closed for a moment, relaxing.

"When I close my eyes, I am praying," Fern-Robin says. "I ask God to show me what you should know about yourself, your past, your future."

"What I *should* know?"

"Yes, sometimes I see things but I also am given to understand that they are not meant for the person to know."

"Why not?"

"Well, in my own case, I had a car accident about a year ago. I had been to readers and not one of them had warned me about driving my car. If someone had seen danger for me while driving, I wouldn't have driven the car. As it turned out, my son was slightly injured in the accident. We took him to the hospital. While X-raying him for the injury, the doctors noticed something much more serious that had nothing to do with the accident. Because they caught it early, we were able to have it successfully treated. Therefore, I believe I was meant to have that accident."

Fern-Robin stares intently into the crystal ball. So do I. I could see nothing in it.

"I always see one image at the beginning. This image represents you and your life. For you I see a star, a lovely shining star. This is very good. It means that your life now is bright and shining and filled with hope. The star also means that your goals are high. But the star is very close to me, not far away. That tells me your goals are not set too high. You have the ability to reach them."

She tells me a great deal about myself, my past, my family and friends, and my work.

"I see a black raven. He is flying around a glass of wine. The raven is trying to get a sip of the wine, but it is a tall glass and he is having trouble. That is a very interesting image. Birds mean freedom to me. With most people, I see birds in cages, trying to escape. But you have found your freedom. You don't want to be too free, however. The wine glass is your home life, your family. You need them and love them very much. You always fly back to them."

She stares into the crystal ball again.

"I see a winged creature. Its wings are very beautiful, like a butterfly. But the wings are not completely open, therefore, it cannot fly very far. The creature is free. Nothing is stopping it from flying. You are the winged creature. You have your wings, you know how to fly. Something is holding you back. Maybe it is worry about your family. Remember, your children are older now. They are beginning to lead their own lives. They don't need you now as much as they did when they were little. You are free to spread your wings and I think you should fly."

I had told Fern-Robin nothing about my children or how old they were.

"Where did you get your crystal?"

"At the Renaissance Festival. A man was selling them. He had a lot of them, all different sizes, on a table. I saw a picture in this one immediately. I looked at others, but I kept coming back to this crystal so I bought it."

"Can you read the tarot cards?"

"No. They have never said anything to me. I can read tea leaves and candle flames and fortune sticks but not the cards. They're just a bunch of pictures to me. But I can read palms."

She reads my palm and we talk about palm reading.

Japanese fortuneteller reading fortune sticks for a client.

9

Palm Reading

$\mathcal{R}$eading the lines in the palm of the hand is an art whose origins are lost in the shadowy past. The earliest mention of this form of fortune-telling is amongst the Chaldeans, a people who lived in ancient Asia. They were experts at palm reading and spread their skill throughout Egypt and India around the eleventh century B.C. Later, palm reading was popular in Greece and Rome. The great teacher Aristotle stated that he could judge how long a man would live by the lines in the hand. He even wrote a paper on the subject whose influence lasted for centuries. Julius Caesar was said to have been an expert palm reader.

Palm reading spread quickly through Europe during the Middle Ages because of the Gypsies, who practiced the art. The Church of the Middle Ages did not approve of palm reading, but considered it much better than other types of fortune-telling.

The popularity of palm reading increased during the Renaissance. An interesting story is told about a well-known palm reader named Colcles who lived in Bologna in the 1490s. Colcles read the palm of a nobleman in the city and told this man he was going to commit a brutal murder. The nobleman did. He was so angry he murdered Colcles!

Look at your own palm. You will see there are many lines on it. If you look closely, however, you will notice that there are probably three major lines with smaller lines around them. To a palm reader, these lines are like footprints in the sand. They tell the reader where the person is going in life and where that person has been.

This old engraving shows the distaste of those times for palm readers.

Young gypsies on the streets of Paris reading palms of passers-by. This was little more than begging, for the reading could not be accurate, and the gypsies would say what they thought a person wanted to hear so they would be given money.

A palm reader will begin by asking if you are right- or left-handed. If you are right-handed, as most people are, the right hand (the working hand) tells where you are in life now. It also reveals your past life. The left hand holds a record of what you were meant to be in life, and it can predict the future. If you are left-handed, the right hand predicts the future and the left hand reveals the present and the past.

Which hand shall it be? Palm reader David A. Kinzie and David Baldwin.

"If the person is ambidexterous—uses both hands equally well—it is awful," Fern-Robin tells me. "You start reading in one hand and then you have to skip to the other. My mother always said she should charge double for that type of person!"

The palm reader not only reads the lines on the palms, he or she looks at the shape of the hand, the length of the fingers, and even the shape of the fingers. A square hand, for example, is the hand of one who works with the hands. A pointed hand is the hand of a dreamer and an artist, while a cone-shaped hand is the hand of a lawyer or doctor.

The three major lines on the palm are the life line, the head line, and the heart line. The life line runs from the side of the palm between the thumb and index finger and ends near the wrist. This line is often misunderstood. Most people believe that a short life line means an early death and a long life line means long life. This is not true. There are many other things the palm reader looks for to predict length of life. A short life line that is very deep may mean a long life. A palm reader searches for other signs as well. Look at your own palm once again. Can you find the life line? You may see lines that look like stars on the life line or lines that make a chain. All of these mean certain things to the palm reader and tell about your life.

The head line starts above the life line and runs from between the life line and the index finger across the hand. This line tells about your mind, your intelligence, and how you deal with life. If the head line is joined together at the beginning with the life line, it means you think things through and move slowly and carefully. A head line that is separated from the life line means you are adventurous.

The heart line is the third major line on the hand. It runs from the bottom of the index finger or the middle finger across the palm to below the little finger. The heart line is the line of love and marriage. If there are lots of little lines running up from the heart line it

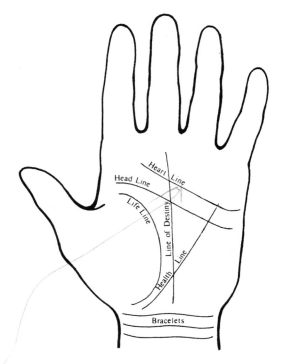

The major lines of the hand.

means you will be happy in love. Lines running down from the heart line mean you will be disappointed.

If the major lines form an "M" shape in the palm, this is considered very lucky and predicts happiness and success in life. If, however, the lines form a five-pointed star in the hand, the Gypsies believed this was a sign the person was a werewolf!

There are many other minor lines on the palm that the reader uses to tell about your life and your future. There are money lines, success lines, fate lines, lines for the number of children you will have, lines for luck. A broken line can mean an accident or a change in jobs or the end of a marriage. A square around a break, however, protects you from any danger the break might cause. A life line that looks like a chain means illness. Stars are signs of good luck.

The palm reader starts by looking at the left hand if the person is right-handed. This hand tells the future or what you were meant to be. Some readers believe in always reading the right hand of a man and the left hand of a woman.

Fern-Robin looks at my left hand. She is startled.

"Look at this," she says, showing me a large break in the life line. "This means you were not meant to live very long."

It is possible to judge years of age on the line, counting around the line from zero at the beginning, like numbers on a clock.

"According to this line, you were not meant to live past twenty or twenty-one. Did you have a serious accident or illness then?"

I tell her I had double pneumonia when I was twenty.

Looking at my right hand, Fern-Robin shows me where the life line had joined together and continued on.

77

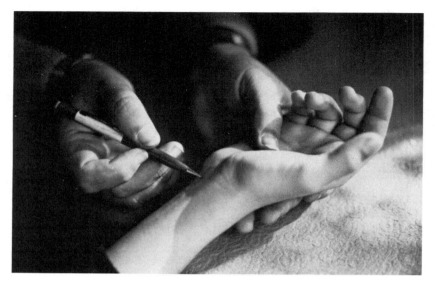

The rings or bracelets of the wrist are read by a palm reader.

"This shows how the future can change," she says. "Here are the marks the illness left, but you decided you were going to live and you did.

"Palm reading is much more exact than card reading or crystal ball gazing. Each line means a certain thing. It tells more about a person physically than the cards or the crystal ball. When my mother reads palms, she sees images in her mind and can tell you even more than the lines on the palm. That is what makes her such a good reader. I just interpret the lines. This line, for example, means you have leadership ability but you don't like to use it. This line means success and money, but you will never be rich."

"Why do people have their fortunes told?" I ask.

"First, I think, for fun or curiosity. Everyone wants to know what their future holds and it is fun to have someone who never saw you before tell you things about your past life that are true. Gamblers come to me and want to know if they are going to be lucky on a certain date. They ask me if they should go to Las Vegas this weekend or wait a week! Sometimes I can see luck and sometimes I can't. If I can't, I tell them."

"Are you always truthful about what you see?"

Fern-Robin hesitates a moment.

"No," she says slowly. "There are times I don't tell the truth—when it would hurt people more than help them. One time my mother and I visited a nursing home for the elderly. Some of the people there were dying. I could see no future at all for them. I didn't tell them that, though. Instead we talked about their pasts. When I look into my crystal ball I see the past in colors. I see your past in greens and browns—earth tones. That means it is alive for you, but you are not living in it. For some people the past is in bright oranges and reds. It means more to them than the present."

"Was there any other time you didn't tell the truth?"

"A young woman came to me. She told me that several years ago she had given up her baby for adoption.

She asked me to tell her what her little girl was doing now, if she was happy and healthy. I had no idea what to say. I could get no image of the child: there was no link between the baby and the mother anymore. But the young woman looked so hopeful. She was hurting inside. So I told her I saw the little girl. She was very happy with her new parents. I told her the child would grow up to be beautiful and beloved. Maybe it was wrong, but when that young woman left me she was happy."

"You really care about the people you read for, don't you?"

"Yes. I enjoy people. I love working festivals. You find out so many interesting things about people. I think that understanding people is the most satisfying part of being a good psychic."

"Do your children have psychic talent?"

"Yes. My little boy can hear voices. That is called *clairaudience*, 'clear hearing.' And I will teach my children what my mother taught me and her grandmother taught her. I have already started them with the fortune sticks the way my mother started me."

And so the gift will be passed on—as it has been for centuries.

Is it clairvoyance? Or is it simply the gift of caring?

Reading the Tea Leaves

*A*ncient peoples believed that evil spirits could be driven away by ringing bells. People hung bells on the roofs of their houses, outside the doors. Then they began to study the insides of the bells for clues to the future. The Chinese believed that teacups were simply bells turned upside down. They studied tea leaves to read the future. As the custom of drinking tea spread, the custom of reading the leaves followed. As with the other fortune-telling arts, reading the tea leaves was brought to Europe by the Gypsys.

Reading the teacup, as it is properly termed, can be fun, and it is certainly easier to learn than reading the tarot or palms. If you are interested in reading fortunes for your friends, this might be a good way to start. The main requirement is a strong imagination and, as in the other branches of fortune-telling, the ability to care for and understand people. Some believe that the reader should be a clairvoyant—like the crystal ball gazer. They feel that the tea leaves and the teacup simply provide a focus point for the clairvoyant to see images that come to the mind—again, much like the crystal ball. Unlike the crystal ball, however, tea leaves really do "form" pictures at the bottom of a tea cup. With some creative thinking, almost anyone can see pictures in the leaves.

First, the Reader prepares tea for the Sitter (the person for whom the reading is being given). It should, of course, be *loose tea* and should be prepared in the

Young Victorian ladies amuse themselves with reading the teacups.

teacup, not in a teapot. The teacup itself is just as important to the reading as the leaves themselves. It should be bell-shaped, white or light-colored, and smooth on the inside. The Sitter drinks the tea, leaving about a teaspoon of tea in the bottom. While drinking, the Sitter should concentrate upon a wish or a question.

The Sitter then takes the cup in his or her left hand. The Sitter swirls the leaves around three times to the left. This distributes the leaves evenly around the cup. The Reader then instructs the Sitter to turn the cup upside down, emptying the remaining tea into the saucer. This should be done carefully, under the Reader's supervision. A person who dumps the tea out of the cup or who shakes the cup will dump most of the leaves out as well.

When the liquid is emptied, the Sitter hands the cup to the Reader. Some of the tea leaves will fall out with the liquid, of course. Those that remain inside the cup form patterns and designs. It is these patterns and designs that the Reader interprets and uses to predict the future.

Over the years, various designs have come to mean certain things. A ring, for example, is an ancient symbol meaning marriage. But in today's world, the Reader may look into the cup and see an airplane. This means unexpected travel.

The pattern or design the Reader sees when first given the cup will be the answer to the Sitter's wish or question. After that, the Reader studies the leaves, which form patterns from the bottom of the cup to the top and all around the sides. The Reader looks at the leaves from many angles and can see many designs.

The handle of the cup represents the Sitter and the home. The reading begins at the left of the handle. These symbols have direct relation to the Sitter at the present time. Designs appearing farther from the handle, as the Reader turns the cup, symbolize events happening in the future. Designs in the leaves at the bottom of the cup represent the distant future. The Reader may see a car, a ring, and a palm tree, for instance. This could mean a fortunate marriage resulting in happiness. A car is good luck, palm trees mean happiness in love or marriage.

Unlike the tarot cards, crystal ball gazing, or palm reading, tea leaves can be, and generally are, read every day. It is also considered perfectly correct for a Reader to read his or her own teacup. The leaves are read each morning and the future predicted for the next twenty-four hours.

Seeing pictures in the leaves is like seeing pictures in clouds. It takes practice not only to see the pictures but to learn how to interpret them for the Sitter. There are books which list the meanings for the pictures. Generally these are simple and easy to understand, unlike the complex tarot cards. Swords, guns, crosses, and coffins are ill omens, for example. Flowers, stars, clovers, and crowns are good omens. If the leaves are cloudy or confused so that the Reader can see no pictures, this represents the mind of the Sitter.

One person who is said to have believed in the tea leaves was the outlaw Jesse James. According to legend, his wife, Zee, was a skilled Reader and read them, not only for Jesse, but his friends as well.

Reading teacups can be fun and entertaining. It is relatively esay to learn. Some of the books listed in the bibliography have lists of designs or patterns and how to interpret them.

Is It True?

*C*an the tarot cards predict your future?

Do pictures really form in the crystal ball?

Can the lines in your hand tell how long you will live?

I don't know.

I enjoyed going to the fortune-tellers. I think all of us like being the center of attention. We love to hear people tell us about ourselves. But it is important to keep a sensible attitude about fortune-telling. There are, unfortunately, some people involved in fortune-telling who are criminals. Unlike the ones I met, these people don't care about anyone but themselves. They take advantage of people.

The police told me about a palm reader who warned her customers that she saw in their hands that they were going to be robbed. She told them to bring her all their money and she would put it in a safe place. Of course, the palm reader left town with her customers' money! The foolish people were left with nothing but the poor comfort of knowing that her predictions had come true. They had, indeed, been robbed!

If you want to have your fortune told, it is important to find a reader you can trust. Many cities now have Renaissance festivals or Psychic Fairs and these are excellent places to have your fortune told. A good occult bookstore can give you the names of several readers, or you might see if there is a Psychical Society or Astrological Society in your city. The psychics I talked to advise

In this famous painting, *The Fortuneteller,* by Georges de La Tour, that dates to 1630, there is a warning against the thievery of some fortune tellers.

that you should avoid fortune-tellers you might see advertising along the highway. In some communities this is actually illegal.

Remember, too, that some readers will not read for those under sixteen. This is why I suggest that young people have their fortunes read at fairs and festivals. *Above all, keep a sensible attitude about the reading.*

If you are interested in further study about the tarot cards or palmistry or any of the other fortune-telling devices mentioned in this book, you will find a list of books in the back which will be of help. You can find many of these at your library or at bookstores, especially occult bookstores. Some bookstores also sell tarot decks.

Some educational institutions offer courses in fortune-telling and the occult sciences. If you are not old enough to attend these courses, you might be able to contact the teachers who are skilled in these arts for further information.

A final word: serious readers truly care about people. They enjoy listening to people and talking to them. Maybe this is the heart of their psychic gifts. Maybe it is because they have opened themselves up to others that they can hear more and see more than the rest of us. If this is part of the psychic gift, then it is a very special gift indeed.

Bibliography

THE TAROT

Blakeley, John D. *The Mystical Tower of the Tarot*. London: Robinson and Watkins Books Ltd., 1974.

Butler, Bill. *Dictionary of the Tarot*. New York: Shocken Books, 1975.

Douglas, Alfred. *The Tarot, the Origins, Meaning and Uses of the Cards*. New York: Taplinger Publishing Co., 1972.

Gray, Eden. *A Complete Guide to the Tarot*. New York: Bantam Books, 1981. (Originally published by Crown Publishers, 1970.)

Hoeller, Stephen A. *The Royal Road, A Manual of Kabalistic Meditations on the Tarot*. Wheaton, Illinois: The Theosophical Publishing House, 1975.

Huson, Paul. *The Devil's Picturebook, A Complete Guide to the Tarot Cards: Their Origins and Their Usage*. New York: G. P. Putnam's Sons, 1971.

PALMISTRY

Sorell, Walter. *The Story of the Human Hand*. New York: Bobbs-Merrill Co., 1967.

Wilson, Joyce. *The Complete Book of Palmistry*. New York: Bantam Books, 1978. (Originally published by Workman Publishing Co., 1971.)

TEA LEAVES

Schapira, Joel, David, and Karl. *The Book of Coffee and Tea*. New York: St. Martin's Press, 1975.

GENERAL

Aylesworth, Thomas G. *Astrology and Foretelling the Future*. New York: Franklin Watts, 1973.

Bizet, Georges. *Carmen*. An Opera in Three Acts by Henri Heilhac and Ludovic Halévy after the novel by Prosper Mérimée. (Many excellent recordings of *Carmen* are available.)

Martin, Kevin. *The Complete Gypsy Fortune Teller*. New York: G. P. Putnam's Sons, 1970.

Miall, Agnes M. *The Book of Fortune Telling*. London: The Hamlyn Publishing Group, Ltd., 1972. (Originally published by C. Arthur Pearson, Ltd., 1951.)

Pelton, Robert W. *Ancient Secrets of Fortune-Telling*. New York: A. S. Barnes and Co., Inc., 1976.

Zolar. *The Encyclopedia of Ancient and Forbidden Knowledge*. New York: Fawcett Popular Library, 1970. (Originally published by Nash Publishing.)

Index